NON-ORGANIC
BEINGS

Mohammad Ali Taheri

First published in Farsi (Persian) in 2011

ISBN-10: 193950712X
ISBN-13: 978-1939507129
LCCN: 2013913370

Interuniversal Press

Contents

Foreword

God created people and set us on the challenging path of the material world to return complete and aware. Throughout our path, people need awareness to face and overcome the elements of test that has been set before us. Without true perception and understanding of these elements, humankind will incur losses that will affect even future generations. Among these elements there is a type of beings that despite their constant encounters with human life, remains largely unidentified and is introduced in this book as "non-organic beings."

Today, the consequences of non-organic beings possessing individuals' minds (*Zehn*) have caused a pandemic of mental problems across the world. Due to the lack of knowledge about these beings and because we lack preventive measures and means of relief from these illness-causing agents' possession, mental disorders have increased.

This book contains considered and relevant theories about non-organic beings and summarizes the last three decades' clinical trials in hopes that, with further research in scientific and medical institutions, we can relieve a considerable amount of humankind's suffering. In addition, this book develops the appropriate understanding and worldview to prevent humankind from making mistakes that put our physical and spiritual life at risk both as individuals and as a society.

Therefore, this book attempts to:

-Explain the role of non-organic beings and prevent disorders they cause.

-Increase motivation for rightful and *Kamal*[1]-oriented life and avoidance of any interactions with these beings.

-Increase attention to the teachings of divine religions.

The next volume will present more comprehensive and thorough views, and solutions offering relief from possession by non-organic beings and recovery from disorders it causes for further research and application by medical practitioners, primarily psychiatrists and psychologists.

Wishing you Divine Grace
Mohammad Ali Taheri

1- Refers to the humankind's spiritual growth toward completion (perfection) and includes self realization and self awareness; meaning clarity of vision and perception about the universe, where we have come from, for what purpose and where we are headed to.

Chapter 1

TYPES OF NON-ORGANIC BEINGS

Non-organic beings are living beings without the live structural components of plants, animals, and humankind (cells, minerals, organic matter) and naturally are not visible, but each type plays a significant role in human life. The inevitable effects of these beings on a person make it impossible to deny their existence, but their concealed role makes identifying them difficult.

This book calls the two main types of non-organic beings "Type A" and "Type B." Their common factor is the ability to possess people's minds so as to cause annoyance, illness and influence their decision making.

Today many people struggle against complications and disorders resulting from these beings' interference in their external affairs (social affairs) and internal affairs (the human mind's management of cells and body's activities, perceptions, and decision making). Despite this predicament's increasing intensity, the current lack of understanding about the role of these beings has not permitted us to seek preventive measures. Therefore, humankind's wellbeing and aspirations have remained in jeopardy.

1- Non-organic Beings: Type A

Research into this type of non-organic beings[1], requires a study of their general and particular characteristics along with familiarity with their relation to the Devil, as that is often questioned.

Differences and Similarities of Type A and the Devil

Type A non-organic beings and Satan or the Devil are often mistaken for one another. Some people think of them as one and believe that Satan is a type A being, is a factor in temptation who is also called the Devil. There are many diverse theories, one of which this book explores and studies.

In this viewpoint, Type A are divine agents, like angels, created with a particular role in the order of the world of existence. Although angels have no free will in playing their role, these beings can decide whether to play theirs. Angels are constituents and laws of existence. They create the backdrop for human being's presence, trial and maturity in the world of duality. In this experience, many elements facilitate human trial and maturity. One of these elements is Type A non-organic beings.

Any divine agent that causes temptation and attraction as a challenge and test for humankind to facilitate our development and growth on the path to *Kamal* can be considered an element of fire[2]. Without this fire, humankind would be left raw and malleable, and with no resistance and opposing forces on our path, our *Kamal* would be meaningless.

Humankind is constantly faced with internal and external fire elements. Internal fire is the collective *Kamal* preventive factors (anti-*Kamal* selves)

1- Also known as Jinn, Djin or Genie.
2- This encounter resembles the firing process in pottery where clay is fired to harden and take the final form for which it is designed.

each of which can be called a "Satan" who is a manifestation of the "Devil" (*Iblis*). The external fire elements we encounter are Type A non-organic beings that play their role in seven different categories. On the basis of their tasks, most of them can also be called "Satan".

As a fire element challenging humankind, the Devil is a Type A non-organic being. Yet as a divine agent who, following a pre-designed plan, played its role in drawing Adam[1] to the scene of challenge and maturity, he can also be considered an angel[2].

Creation manifests precise and specific planning fulfilled by angels (laws of existence). In the cycle of the world of duality, every angel has a specific function that ends at a precise position in Adam's return to the final point of the cycle. In other words, in our return route, Adam triumphs over angels[3] (laws) one after the other at specific points of the cycle.

The observer at the final point of the cycle, which is in a time-free state[4], observes the entire process at once. However, before the observer can triumph over the dominance of time, the truth of this journey can only be seen gradually and in fragments.

Among these divine agents, only the Devil's role continues through the end of the cycle. Adam will not dominate the Devil--that is, the Devil does not bow to Adam--until the last point in the cycle. This phenomenon occurs because the Devil is this cycle's element of duality. Without duality (good and evil) and free will -Adam's choice and growth in the direction of *Kamal*- would be meaningless.

Considering this essential factor, the truth of the story of the creation

---

1- Adam represents all humankind that ever existed and will exist in the future. Adam refers to all humanity.

2- Angels Are pillars of existence that execute laws of existence creating a set for humankind's growth.

3- In other words: Angels bow to Adam

4- The state of timelessness where humankind dominates time.

of Adam and the Devil's disobedience becomes apparent. It would be a mistake to consider the Devil's refusal to bow to Adam as outside the plan of creation and the Devil as a super power that defied the Creator's will and caused duality. It would be a mistake to think that the Devil imposed his will on the Creator, causing duality. That would be a mistake because it would set the Devil as ultimate evil against God as ultimate good, which is an obvious *shirk*[1].

Based on divine wisdom, creating the cycle of the world of duality required a duality factor (angel that runs the law of duality), and the Devil took this role. So although not bowing to Adam may seem like the Devil's rebellion against the plan of creation, it is in fact in accordance with the plan. Without disobedience there would have been no duality.

However, the story most obviously demonstrates that arrogance and defiance caused the Devil to be exiled from the world of unity. That lesson holds for the entire journey of the cycle of duality: like the Devil, who descended from the world of unity to the world of duality, humankind's arrogance would distance us from unity and drive us to multiplicity. If humankind does not recognize that thinking "I am better than he" was what distanced the Devil from unity, we will pass through the entire cycle with the same pride and arrogance and see ourselves as higher than God. In this case, in the last test of the cycle a person will still prefer himself to God and thus fail the test and not experience Heaven in unity.

In this segment of duality, each person has numerous manifestations of the Devil that can be considered his inner Satans. Essentially, considering the duality cycle as a whole, we see Adam continually opposed by the Devil. Given the numerous manifestations of Adam and the Devil, people are repeatedly opposed by inner Satans, each of which is

---

1- Equating anything to God

an indestructible part of our being. Yet if an individual can control and manage these inner Satans and harness them, he will be on the path to *Kamal*. Therefore, these inner Satans (anti-*Kamal* selves) are contributing factors to humankind's maturity and growth.

It is because of these anti-*Kamal* selves that humankind can go astray from the path of *Kamal*. It is because of these anti-*Kamal* selves that we can commit an offense for the sake of our children, wealth, and comfort or grabbing opportunities. Our interests are our external motives, but it is the inner anti-*Kamal* selves that create attachment to them, tempt us toward rebellion and are the inner possibilities of these acts. It is these inner Satans' voice that drive us to negative thoughts, actions, and feelings. However, Type A beings, manifesting divine wisdom and justice through seven different tasks, are external factors that test humankind.

General Characteristics of Type A Non-organic Beings

In universal ecology, numerous beings exist, each serving a specific purpose. One such type exists in the natural life on the Earth and plays its role in the physical part of humankind's life. The other is designed to contribute to the quality of humankind's life. Each type has a distinct purpose in humankind's aspirations and on our path to *Kamal*.

Each person must navigate and track his path to *Kamal* despite all obstacles, and Type A can be considered part of the setting and backdrop of our path to *Kamal*. Therefore, this type of non-organic beings has pre-defined roles in humankind's journey toward *Kamal*.

They are invisible, non-physical beings capable of revealing themselves in any form they choose to an individual under suitable circumstances (when the individual creates the basis). Like humankind, these beings mate, die, and have intelligence. However, one of the most important differences between them and humankind is that they do not benefit from step of love outcomes such as enthusiasm, happiness, astonishment, kindness, sacrifice, and intuition.

Therefore, unlike humankind who is created and designed for an immense transformation in the world of duality, eventually attaining an actual state from a potential state (that is, reaching unity), these beings were created to experience no such huge transformation. Like other life forms, they can experience only limited change within their defined life framework.

Their intelligent processing is limited to decision making within the scope of their role in the material world. In the physical world, each being bears a consciousness that can be called its intelligence. The intelligence of an atom is the background (setting) of its existence. An ant has its own form of intelligence, too. But an ant has not only background intelligence, but also vital and instinctual intelligences that facilitate a life based on instincts.[1]

Type A non-organic beings also have intelligence. Apart from background, vital and instinctive logic intelligences, they also possess logic intelligence that enables them to make conscious decisions. This intelligence is not at the same level of humankind's free will, but it separates them from other beings possessing only lower level intelligences.

Type A beings process data to the extent that they can plan how to complete their tasks. Their understanding of what humankind knows does not result from their own data processing and intellectual analysis, but often comes from people. Their knowledge of matters and events of which people are unaware, results from their ability to very rapidly ap-

---

1- This is based on the author's description of six stages of creation consisting of Fundamental Vibration Consciousness, Background Consciousness, Vital Consciousness, Instinctive Logic Consciousness, Logic Consciousness, and Love Consciousness.

pear in different locations.

These beings also lack the ultra-mind awareness threshold, never becoming inspired. Therefore, they cannot be creative or innovative. These abilities are acquired only on the step of love, to which these beings have no access. In other words, Type A beings do not have the ability to penetrate into supreme consciousness (divine knowledge) because they do not need to access such level of awareness to play their pre-defined role.

In Type A beings, psychological structure is different from that of humankind. The human psyche (psychological body) has two sections, instinctive psyche and emotional psyche, while all other living beings possess only instinctive psyche. For instance, if a rat's food is put in a glass box where the rat can see but not reach it, the rat will suffer depression after a period of unsuccessful struggle to reach the food. This psychological reaction in animals (sadness, stress, anxiety) that can also lead to psychosomatic disorders derives from their instinctive psyche. Plants also have instinctive psyche. For instance, when cattle begin eating grass on one side of a field, grass on the other side becomes bitter. This process is not a conscious process but occurs naturally and instinctively.

In addition to this instinctive psyche, human psyche has an emotional psyche element that responds to mental data processing. That is, a person's perception of events and behaviors that he encounters affect his emotional psyche and determine its reactions. But Type A non-organic beings, like all beings other than humankind, have no emotional psyche.

The life span of Type A beings varies up to several hundred years, depending on their role. They reproduce, and their relationship with their children is like that of animals; that is, the child is dependent upon the mother for survival for a period of time and is on its own thereafter.

These being's mating rules are also similar to those of animals, making monogamy or polygamy irrelevant. Unlike humankind, who find marriage significant in the path of *Kamal*, Type A non-organic beings mate simply in response to their sexual urge and instinctive inclinations.

Humankind's libido has not only an instinctive basis but also a mental processing base. The intensity of this drive and its timing depend upon such processing and are manageable. However, in Type A beings, this drive emerges from no such processing and is not selective. These beings, usually a category of these beings in charge of tempting humankind, can mate with human beings.

Type A beings feed from a form of energy and are more dilute than physical matter. Although they can become visible by changing their vibration frequency, make physical contact, and even move objects, they need neither physical food nor physical objects. They obtain their energy from nature but if they possess a human being, they can feed from his chakras and energy transformers. This process harms the infected individual because over time his organs and tissues suffer deficient vital force, eventually causing illness in the affected areas. In such cases alternative therapies such as acupuncture, cupping, or venesection have provided short-term solutions by causing Type A beings to temporarily leave the energy channels. Non-organic beings are not compatible with the magnetic field of metals (needles or blades), and these or similar methods rid the energy channels of these viruses for a period of time, usually about six months.

Table 1 describes similarities and differences between Type A non-organic viruses and humankind.

Table 1. Comparison of Type A Non-organic Beings and Humankind

ABILITY	TYPE A	HUMANKIND
LOVE DERIVATIVES	NO	YES
INTELLIGENCE	YES	YES
LOGICAL INTELLIGENCE	NO	YES
CREATIVITY	NO	YES
FREE WILL	YES	YES
PHYSICAL ACTIVITIES	YES	YES
REPRODUCTION	YES	YES
TELEPORTATION	YES	NO
CHANGE OF FORM & APPEARANCE	YES	NO
CHANGE OF FREQUENCY	YES	NO
NEED FOR PHYSICAL OBJECTS	NO	YES
ILLNESS	NO	YES
FOOD	ENERGY	PHYSICAL FOOD
MATING	YES	YES
IMITATION	YES	YES
TENDENCY FOR DOMINATION	YES	YES
LUST	INSTICTIVE	INSTICTIVE AND EMOTIONAL
CREATION OF TOOLS	NO	YES
JEALOUSY	NO	YES
TENDENCY TO LIE	YES	YES
PREFERENCE FOR PHYSICAL BEAUTY	NO	YES
NEED FOR TECHNOLOGY	NO	YES
BIRTH AND DEATH	YES	YES
ASPIRATION	YES	YES

Categories of Type A Non-organic Beings (Based on Their Role)

Type A non-organic beings play atleast seven distinct roles as categorized below:

A_1: Universe Keepers

A_2: Trial Keepers

A_3: Direction Keepers

A_4: Wisdom Keepers

A_5: Retribution Keepers

A_6: Spell Keepers

A_7: Captivation Keepers

A_1: Universe Keepers

This category of non-organic beings is called Universe Keepers because they guard the material world. Every element of existence is an emanation, a manifestation, a name, and an image of its Creator, and is thus sacred. In response to desecration of any part of the universe, Universe Keepers attack the offender and penetrate his mind. This system leads to the development and maturity of humankind. Violation of an element of the universe has many dimensions, including the unnecessary breaking of a tree branch or disrespecting a person in any way, such as false accusation or passing judgment on someone in their absence.

Nature's sacredness is such that humankind cannot destroy it to fulfill their natural needs. Humankind can benefit from nature based on natural laws and principles while respecting the ecosystem and its biodiversity. This phenomenon has an optimal level without going to extremes. For instance, it is natural to feed upon other beings based on the ecosystem food chain. However, that natural law does not permit humankind to hunt and take an animal's life for their amusement and pleasure. If one slaughters a sheep to feed the poor or those in need, that act remains within the boundaries of the food chain. However, if one kills a sheep for a ritual or a superstitious notion of obtaining health or prosperity by this sacrifice, that act constitutes a desecration to the material world, and Universe Keepers then take action.

When Universe Keepers intervene, they attack the offender, capture his mind, and cause various mental, psychological, and physical disorders. For instance, they use the individual's vital energy and cause illness over time. Additionally, within the boundaries of their free will, Universe Keepers can plan the manner in which they take control over the individual's free will or cause any sort of distress. They consider his interests and inclinations and cause him appropriate suffering. For instance, if hygiene is significant to him, they will cause him obsessive compulsive cleaning disorder. Alternatively, they may infuse a false and persistent fear (phobia), hallucination, and other disorders that are discussed in Chapter Two of this book.

Human perceptions and our level of awareness of our own unjustness are not defining factors of this retribution. Thus, even if someone commits an injustice without being aware of the precise definition of the word, he will encounter this category of non-organic beings because recognizing good and evil is in human nature, and he knows without being told or taught that breaking a tree is wrong.

A₂: Trial Keepers

This category of Type A non-organic beings are responsible for establishing test conditions for humankind. They reveal the strength or weakness of the faith of two groups: those who claim to have faith in the truth and those who take pride in their faith and ability to control their desires. Great people of faith like prophets constantly encountered this category of non-organic beings who offered them help, power, wealth, and other temptations to test their faith.

Often people who are confident and proud of their chastity encounter such beings in the form of an attractive person that will attempt to seduce them to test that chastity. Certain individuals value contact with a saint or spiritual person who appears in a very graceful manner. Generally, the individual becomes greatly influenced by this being (actually a Trial Keeper) who becomes the center of his trust and faith. The individual considers the emergence of the Trial Keeper as a result of his faith and therefore begins attracting people toward himself, thus breaking the agreement of "Move directly toward Him."

The moment a person feels religious arrogance and pride in having strong faith, Trial Keepers become involved. Often, contrary to some individuals' confidence in their own faith, Trial Keepers' involvement reveals the weakness of their beliefs. Satan's role is to use this weakness of faith and create diversion. The individual's diversion of attention and submission results from his weakness because following a Trial Keeper is choosing to be its slave. Some individuals not only rely on Trial Keepers but also create a spiritual explanation and justification for their choice.

The basis and the manner of Trial Keepers' challenges are unforeseeable because they can create test circumstances in different ways. In the journey of life humankind encounters many natural tests. But tests created by Trial Keepers are not for ordinary people but for those who are taking the path of *Kamal*, growing faith, or are confident at any level of faith they possess.

A₃: Direction Keepers

Humankind needs direction to find a route that leads him to *Kamal*. If this course is not set to a straight path toward God and humankind puts his hope, trust, and faith in anything or anyone besides God, he is lost. In this case he is in *Shirk*, he reveres a source other than God and has broken the agreement of "We seek help (for each and everything), only (and absolutely) from You." When humankind deviates from the straight path to God, a category of Type A non-organic beings called Direction Keepers attack and intervene.

This attack can occur without the individual noticing it, hiding the cause of his discomfort and annoyance. For instance, individuals who have strayed from the straight path suffer from depression and psychological disorders instead of feeling peace and contentment that result from God's presence.

During the circular walk around *Kaaba* in the *Hajj* pilgrimage, a pilgrim's direction should not be diverted to the left or right. This religious practice conveys a message and a lesson: the importance of constantly looking straight toward God with no diversion. This lesson is important because people who have not set their course aligned with this straight path remain outside divine protection and are vulnerable to harm.

Even the slightest *shirk* results in an encounter with Direction Keepers and the torment they cause. The degree of *shirk* and its repetition determines the severity of this torment. They enter when a person opens the gate, and remain even after the gate closes, but a person with a constantly open gate remains in greater distress.

A person's inner fire element (inner Satan) continuously leads him to anything other than God. Therefore, if its means of deception are not recognized and controlled, it will cause deviation from the straight path and open the gate for Direction Keepers' intervention. Thus, a person falls into torment caused by his own unawareness.

A4: Wisdom Keepers

Wisdom Keepers are a category of Type A non-organic beings who play a role in managing divine wisdom. God attributes a person's guidance and depravity to himself. The main law that manages divine wisdom is "the law of reflection[1]" and its basis is an individual's inner yearnings and desires. The divine agents that fulfill humankind's negative inner yearnings by their intervention and cause deviation are called Wisdom Keepers.

Individuals with an inclination for negativity attract Wisdom Keepers. As a fire element, Wisdom Keepers play their role and answer the individual's inner desire for negativity. On the one hand, they create conditions that lead humankind to depravity, and on the other hand, they impel us to say and to do things that put us in misery. In other words, they create a kind of foolishness in the individual that drives him to say and do foolish things. Another way in which Wisdom Keepers fulfill their responsibility is to inspire. For instance, they instill a sense of arrogance and superiority in an individual, and that arrogance causes his collapse.

Humankind is not aware of the details or the manner in which the law of reflection manages divine wisdom. For instance, one of the rewards of positive inner desires is love. The timing and manner of the experience of love are not by choice; that is, it does not flow from a person's decision and awareness of the manner of its occurrence. It is divine wisdom that drives a person to experience love to achieve a level of *Kamal* and maturity.

Moreover, when divine wisdom requires a Wisdom Keeper to play the role of answering a person's negative desires, that role is beyond human will or choice. This being only leads the individual to circumstances that correspond with his negative thoughts, words, and actions (negative inner desires). Therefore, this category of Type A beings, contrary to Trial Keepers, do not operate by human invitation or suggestion.

1- Humankind have a radiation of our being that results from our thoughts, words and actions. This radiation can be positive or negative. An individual's radiation to the higher realm is amplified and then echoed to the positive or negative networks to reflect back on the individual. Therefore what a person receives is an amplification of his own being.

A₅: Retribution Keepers

The internal states of humankind can be categorized into two main groups: positive and negative. Positive states include feelings of hope, happiness, and calm, whereas negative states comprise destructive feelings such as fear, guilt, anxiety, loneliness, and sadness. Being in a negative state underlies many psychological, mental, mentosomatic, and psychosomatic disorders[1]. Such outcomes occur because in this state, a category of Type A non-organic beings called Retribution Keepers can penetrate a person's mind and cause these illnesses. Humankind's maturity and *Kamal* bring us under the "Divine Forces," causing positive feelings and a positive state. However, if an individual experiences the second group of feelings for any reason, he has fallen under "Satanic Forces," and so Retribution Keepers influence his mind.

Further, committing any offenses[2] emits negative radiation that attracts Retribution Keepers. Although the offender may be in a state of calm and happiness, the negative radiation emission attracts this category of non-organic beings. In this instance, the offense is not being in a negative state. It is essential that while remaining in a positive state, humankind utilize these feelings in the path to *Kamal* and in the direction of positive thoughts and actions, and not commit an offense in a state of happiness, contentment, and calm.

Therefore, a person's encounter with Retribution Keepers may begin in a negative psychological state or a positive state wherein he commits an offense. This category of non-organic beings can cause retribution in different forms, similar to Universe Keepers and Direction Keepers. However, their role in managing divine retribution is of great importance.

"Divine Retribution" occurs by various natural laws in the material world. For instance, the collective consciousness radiation of all hu-

---

1- See Chapter 3 for more details about negative and positive states.
2- An offence or sin is comitting any act that leads a person in the direction of anti-Kamal

mankind affects the entire material world and can change and determine its form. If this result is negative, its response from the material world is negative for all. This negative response that results from the overall offenses of human society puts all living beings in an unpleasant condition and represents divine retribution.

In addition, the evolution of civilizations in human societies has caused an increasing tendency toward imposing forms of order that increase human conflict with the natural world. This desire for extreme order causes a rebellion of the subconscious part of the human mind against order. This rebellion in turn causes increasing social disorder such as vandalism and robbery and personal inclinations toward sadistic and masochistic behavior. In other words, disregarding natural laws (such as the universe's law of order and disorder[1]) creates problems that can also be considered divine retribution.

Any disturbance caused by Type A non-organic beings, on the basis of their role in the material world and resulting from humankind's wrongdoing, is a form of divine retribution. Among these, the Retribution Keepers' intervention reveals divine retribution. These disturbances may include arousing various kinds of compulsive and obsessive behaviors, hallucinations, paranoia, and multiple personality disorder. They may also cause annoyance by misplacing or loss of a person's belongings. The misplacing of objects can also occur from intervention by Captivation Keepers or by any Type A non-organic being who imitates humankind in using physical objects.

These beings can also possess a person's mind and cause an individual to move an object to an unlikely and inappropriate location from which he has difficulty retrieving the object when needed.

1- The reality of the material world appears with disorder and the truth of it reflects order. Hence the world of existence is created from order and disorder.

A₆: Spell Keepers

This category of non-organic beings become active for casting spells. They become active in different ways with the involvement of the negative network[1]. The negative network can also directly cast spells that cause damage in the form of negative radiation without the use of these beings. Spell Keepers activate spells that are cast with the help of mental or written codes or formulas. Intentional or unintentional use of these codes grants these beings the capability of executing them and sets them on a specific mission. These codes may be used in the form of a specific table of numbers, alphabets, mantras, or images and symbols. Figure 1 depicts the operation of spells.

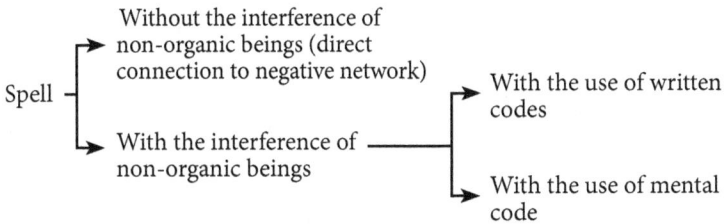

Figure 2. Operation of Spells

For overall prevention of entanglement with any form of spells, humankind must remain in positive states such as hope, peace, and happiness, and avoid negative states such as fear, sorrow, and anxiety. Although participation in casting spells (with good or bad intentions) is immoral, by not taking safety measures, the victim creates the conditions for the spell to be cast and is thus also responsible for this predi-

---

1- As we live in the world of duality and everything finds its meaning with its opposite (for instance, good and bad, high and low, day and night), there also exist negative consciousness and positive consciousness that influence the humankind's journey to Kamal. They are called by the author as positive network (positive consciousness) and the negative network (negative consciousness). The negative network provides all the necessary information and awareness that can distract and distance us from the path towards Kamal.

cament. Therefore, the possibility of spells and the existence of Spell Keepers can be considered a collective test for human society.

A₇: Captivation Keepers

Techniques exist for captivating Type B and this category of Type A non-organic beings. Captivation Keepers are tamed and captivated by people who wish to use them and set them on designated missions to which the people assign them. Therefore, they can be called Captivation Keepers.

People can perform such captivation by various methods such as imprisoning their children or threatening to burn or otherwise harm them. People involved in such acts may be attacked by these beings, and their families and future generations may even be disturbed by these beings and face serious consequences.

People can unintentionally activate Spell Keepers by using publicly accessible codes, but people can activate Captivation Keepers only through intentional measures, not necessarily requiring spells.

Type A Non-organic Beings and Religion

The Role of Type A Beings in Purgatory

From a time-free perspective, all segments of the world of duality are consistently connected to one another. Bearing in mind that they take form from unity to multiplicity, as a whole, they look like a tree. Humankind and all other parts of this tree begin taking form from unity and each takes a route to their "Lord"[1].

Because purgatory (a segment of the duality cycle) is an experience in a time-free state, by entering this stage of the cycle, humankind en-

---

1- The term used as an equivalent to the Arabic word Rabb (رب)

counters this live tree. The tree is a testimony of our experience. Where a person encounters a blazingly clear realization of how he has taken the journey of duality up to that point as opposed to how he should have taken it. As humankind enters heaven (the next segment of the duality cycle), the role of the tree for humankind is completed. Similarly, all other elements of the tree return to their Lord along a separate route but parallel to humankind's return to our Lord.

A component of this tree is Type A non-organic beings that, given their nature of fire, are the maturing factor of humankind in life and a burning element in purgatory. Based on their responsibilities, they can be serious threats to humankind for our wrongdoings. Therefore, they become maturation and growth elements for a person who can immune himself from these threats and free himself from them.

These external fire elements accompany humankind in purgatory. In this time-free state, our offenses are present before us and create in us a strong sense of burning regret. In purgatory, humankind witnesses how Universe Keepers' role reveals our depravity (desecration of any part of the material world), Direction Keepers' task disclosed our negligence of the unity of the material world, Wisdom Keepers' responsibility exposed our aberrations, and Trial Keepers' role exposed our preference of pleasure, power, wealth, and fame over our faith. The hardship and bitterness of purgatory is permeated by Trial Keepers' seduction and humankind's ignorance.

The Role of Religion in Exposing Satan and Offering Protection from It

Humankind's understanding of God has had an evolving process and has progressed through time. We first sought God in nature and bowed to the sun, fire, or any other phenomenon that we found powerful, and worshipped it. We then sought God, our unknown powerful Creator, in self-made symbols made of wood, stone, and other materials, and worshipped them.

With the emergence of monotheistic religions, these physical symbols became less popular, and humankind turned to an unseen God. Yet, for us God still had a human form, and until monotheistic prophets changed that figure, we worshipped this human image of an unseen God. With time, God became an unseeable Creator who nonetheless possessed attributes that could describe Him. Though, essentially, His infinite being is indescribable and unperceivable and has no labels or describable characteristics. The attributes that divine religions ascribe to Him only explain the quality of His relationship to the material world. Therefore, acknowledgement of an indescribable and nameless God is the final stage of humankind's evolution of understanding God.

In each phase, alongside our attention to the Creator that is the positive aspect of our curious eye, we also observed the magical powers of nature that are the negative aspect of this curiosity. Thus, the practices of witchcraft as well as the records of humankind's inclination to worship are as old as human history. In addition to our God-seeking nature, humankind has inner capacities for both vice and virtue. Therefore, we observes our world from two different perspectives, *Kamal* and anti-*Kamal*.

The purpose of religion is to serve humankind. From the beginning of time, religions were not distinguishable as divine or satanic. Humankind's first creative and spiritual inspirations were the birth of religion. Yet as water is pure and refreshing at the headspring but may taste different after running for a long distance, with passage of time, religions have become polluted with division, distortion, and deviation. The essence of religion is pure, but with time it finds positive and negative applications.

Throughout the process of seeking God, humankind has been invited by prophets, saints, and mystics to a single religion. There is only one manner[1] that leads to *Kamal,* and that is the manner of submission and surrender. The call for this manner was to help humankind to recognize where to invest our mental, spiritual, and physical assets. Generally the purpose of religion was to aid humankind to see our place in the material world, to answer our primary and fundamental questions, to warn us against obstacles and threats on our path, to show us what to turn toward and what to turn away from. In essence, religions set forth the notion of worship[2] and refrainment from *Taghut*[3].

Religion suggests direction and guidelines, but each individual interprets it in a different way. As a consequence, followers of religions, with division and denying one another, have left the purpose of religions unfulfilled. The message of each prophet is not separated from the others. Each of them has introduced religion to humankind from a unique outlook and emphasized one of humankind's infinite dimensions and potentials, and taught one aspect of divine awareness. To attain divine awareness, we need all these teachings and cannot cast aside a single message[4].

One important service religions have done for humankind has been creating awareness about avoiding non-organic beings. For instance, in

---

1- The author considers religion as affecting one's manners. A person's religion is also his manners based on his beliefs.

2- Humankind's aspiration is to reach Kamal. For instance, an apple tree's seed aspires to germinate, grow into a tree, blossom, and produce apples. To achieve its aspiration, the seed needs a set of inputs and a guideline. If it follows the guideline, it achieves its aspiration. Humankind has received guidelines to achieve our aspiration. To follow those guidelines to reach Kamal is the practice of worship.

3- Means rebellion. There are two categories of elements of rebellion: inner and outer rebellion elements (fire) that persuade people to rebel.

4- For instance, Moses talks about the step of logic and presents commandments, Jesus teaches about the step of love and raises the quality of worship, and Mohammad (as) talks about The Compassionate and The Merciful and invites humankind to reason and logic, and therefore our invitation is for a life with the combination of the two steps, love and logic).

the Bible we find ample information and guidelines about exorcism and the healing of manic individuals (possessed by non-organic beings). This may be the reason that Quran (the next collection of divine guidelines) only briefly mentions these facts.

Religious guidelines ask humankind to avoid following (inner and outer) Satan. Satan's invitation may be by force, by temptation and suggestion, or in some instances a mere hint. Encountering Satan (inner and outer) is based on a set of laws and principles. Once humankind seeks truth and chooses to fulfill our aspiration, Satan begins to challenge us. When humankind seeks true awareness and understanding of the material world and the essence of creation, it is Satan's responsibility to challenge us. It is here that we seek refuge from Satan in God. It is here that, to gain awareness of the truth and to attain *Kamal*, all humankind needs is divine protection from Satan's attacks. Divine religions have repeatedly emphasized this matter.

2- Non-organic Beings: Type B (Mind Bodies)

From an Interuniversal outlook, every person has numerous bodies, such as the physical body, "astral" body, "psychological" body, and "mind" body. Among them there is a body called the "collective spirit" body shared by all humankind, and because of it all people have an invisible connection to one another. Therefore, we consider that all people share each other's fall or rise to *Kamal*.

With a person's death and an end to life in this world, the physical body is separated from the other bodies and begins to decompose, break up into its constituent parts and return to ecosystem. Death also eliminates other human bodies such as the psychological and astral bodies. However, a person's mind body lives on after death.

After death, a person is free from emotional processes and reactions that result from the processing of psychological body software such as feelings of sadness, pain, and happiness. However, because of a deceased individual's attachments to our experiences and memories during his life in this world stored in the mind body's "memory and data archive," he recreates them in his mind that lives on and exhibits emotional behavior. Therefore, the effects of data from the psychological body on the mind body before death are similar to the effects of data that is reread by the surviving mind and become the roots of the individual's decisions and behavior in his life after death.

Death takes place in two stages: physical death followed by absolute death. During physical death stage, a person's astral body is still alive and he can return to life. Absolute death occurs only when the astral body dies. The time difference between physical and absolute death vary from a few minutes to a few days in different people. During this time, any shock to the astral body can revive the physical body. But when the astral body dies, the psychological body also dies, and the only part that lives on is the mind body.

An individual who lives under the management of his mind body after his absolute death is called "mind body," a term equivalent to the word "soul" or "spirit" by which most people mean a deceased human being. On the basis of this lexicon, mind bodies (persons who have experienced absolute death and are now experiencing the next phase are called "Non-organic Beings Type B," and only the guiding soul (Similar to a compass it offers directions to human on his path to *Kamal*) is called "soul".

Throughout humankind's journey in the cycle of the world of duality, our guiding soul is in charge of guiding us toward *Kamal*. For the duration of humankind's life in this world, the guiding soul plays this role by creating in us a feeling of having lost something. With this feeling, each person continues searching for his lost component that is not fulfilled by achieving wealth, education, marriage, and the like. In other words, the guiding soul is the reason humankind finds all earthly pleasures empty. Otherwise, humankind would feel satisfied and happy with the fulfillment of our material desires and would no longer seek *Kamal*. Unlike earthly pleasures, satisfaction of *Kamal* has no end and is constantly desired

Mind Body and Attachment to Life in this World

With an individual's absolute death, when his mind body is about to break away, all that occurred in his life flashes before him in an instant with accurate details, and his attachments in life surface and catch his attention. Thus, when mind body detaches from other elements, it experiences two pulling forces. One is the guiding soul that invites the mind body to go forward and move to the next phase, and the other is the mind body's (positive or negative) ties to life that pull him back and engage him in life in this world.

The mind body's attachments can be to children, spouse, belongings, wealth, power, fame, and the like. Many mind bodies may have strong bonds with this world to the extent that they cannot accept their death for a long time and even imagine a body for themselves.

The experience of death is very sweet for everyone. Even the most horrifying death is not difficult and painful for the person who is experiencing it. That moment is in fact very pleasant. It is the mental attachments to this life and this world that determine the difficulties of death. If one experiences pain and suffering, it results from the individual's ties pulling him back to continue life in this world and his unfamiliarity with the next phase of the journey. Only people who attain knowledge of *Kamal* during their life in this world and enjoy a level of awareness about humankind's return to our Lord welcome death with open arms. After death, uncaring about this life, they move to the next stage of their journey and toward their Lord. In contrast, people who commit suicide remain imprisoned by this world longer than others.

Developing strong bonds is directly related to the alignment of a person's life purpose. Anything that becomes a person's purpose other than *Kamal* becomes an attachment factor. Even means of achieving *Kamal* such as science, religion, spirituality, or mysticism can become a person's distraction if not identified as means for the journey to *Kamal*. For instance, if a person is particular about late night prayers and is involved with that action to the extent that he neglects the quality of that prayer, the means becomes the goal and thus a distraction. Many people are strongly attached to certain actions (negative or positive), to certain people and locations, or even to collections of their favorite objects. When death occurs and all of life's events and experiences are reviewed in the dying person's mind in a split second, these attachments are highlighted. The mind body will tend to return to those ties and live as if death has not occurred. If family is the strongest attachment, the deceased individual will try to live with them as if he were still alive. He will even try to communicate with them and show them that he is still alive and wishes to continue living with them as before. The family or friends sometimes feel a presence, and often this attachment results in the deceased person's mind body possessing the minds of the family members.

Certain people perform the immoral act of communicating with mind bodies. A study of these communications reveals several points worth discussing. If a mind body is present when called, it demonstrates its continuing ties to this life, its desire to make its presence known, and its hesitation to move forward. Some of these mind bodies are constantly present and may even introduce themselves as someone else who has been summoned by these communications. They are commonly called "wandering souls." These mind bodies who refuse to move forward from limbo seek any opportunity to make their presence known. They can possess the mind of a living individual. They usually look for someone who has similar inclinations or attachments so that they can experience this world through the window of that person's mind. However, if a mind body has achieved knowledge of *Kamal*, it will not miss the opportunity to move forward to the next phase of the journey to perfection. As a result, elevated mind bodies cannot be summoned or contacted, and people who claim to be in contact with the saints or uplifted souls are in fact being deceived by other non-organic beings.

Mind bodies are keen to correspond and report their present state because of their strong ties to a person or an entity. These reports are based on the mind body's imagination formed by these attachments and can occur in reality or in a dream. For instance, the mind body of a priest, due to strong devotion to his job, may constantly imagine himself holding his holy book, going to the church and performing the religious rituals just as he did before death. If the person witnessing the report is not aware of the drastic changes in the conditions of life after death, he may believe that the deceased priest is giving accurate information about his new environment, whereas the priest is actually imprisoned by his attachments to his life before death and cannot move forward. Some mind bodies describe themselves as happy in a beautiful garden. Many of people who hear of such stories believe that this person has found his way to heaven although, in fact, the mind body is in that state only in its imagination and in response to its mental attachment. Such a description could be due to its love for nature, expectation of going to heaven, or the long lost dream of living in a garden that was not fulfilled during life before death.

In any case, humankind's attachments not only affect the quality of our life in this world, but they can also restrain us from experiencing what is essential in our path to *Kamal*.

Why Death Was Designed in the Plan of Creation

In the cycle of the world of duality, while people can achieve all levels of *Kamal* with our free will and ability to choose, experiencing each stage of this cycle causes a different kind of *Kamal* for us that is beyond our free will and is based on the plan of creation. This form of *Kamal* achieved as a result of the reduction of humankind's existential dimensions is a journey from neediness to absolute needlessness through the phenomenon called "death."

Reaching the state of needlessness may seem possible in the stage of living in this world, but we must realize that we can achieve only a certain level of it in this world because humankind has many existential elements and dimensions. Such components are essential to sustain life in this world, but we leave them behind with death. These elements entail certain needs; therefore, we cannot achieve needlessness in this stage of duality. For instance, a newborn is at his highest point of neediness and cannot live without his parents' care, but as the baby grows older, new needs replace those of infancy. Now the question becomes: even if this person lives for 1000 years, will he ever reach needlessness? It is important to consider that even someone with an ascetic lifestyle still requires a minimal amount of food to live. Thus, an eternal life in this world is equivalent to eternal neediness and denies *Kamal,* the journey from neediness to absolute needlessness. Therefore, God has blessed humankind with death in our path, so that shifting to the next state reduces our neediness. In other words, the basis of death is divine love, and it guarantees that humankind returns to God.

In addition, death enables people to experience a different form of journey to *Kamal* without having to attend to our physical needs. If death were a matter of choice, not only would most people not have chosen to leave this world, but most of us would also have spent our entire lives attending to our physical needs and ignored *Kamal*.

Humankind constantly experiences two inviting forces. One is an upward pulling force (*Kamal*), and the other is a downward pulling force (anti-*Kamal*). In this life, worldly possessions and humankind's pride (self-importance) constitute the anti-*Kamal* force that distracts and engages us with worldly affairs. The feeling of being lost or having lost something (that is not fulfilled by earthly pleasures) invites us in the direction of seeking *Kamal*.

These forces exist after death in a different form. The anti-*Kamal* force is humankind's attachments to life before death that stops us from shifting to the next state (space-free world) and the *Kamal* force is the guiding soul that invites us to move forward to that next world. The intensity of humankind's attachments defines our suspense in limbo after death. By overcoming the anti-*Kamal* force, humankind can move forward to a new birth in the new world[1].

1- This does not refer to reincarnation. Please see the author's assessment of reincarnation in chapter 2.

SYMPTOMS AND DISORDERS CAUSED BY NON-ORGANIC BEINGS

Non-organic beings can take over a person's commanding unit (mind) so as to gain control and influence over him. They consume people's vital energy by taking hold of our chakras and energy channels and act as parasites.

By violating a person's mind, these beings can interfere in memory management and data arranging management units and, in an obvious or subliminal manner, project their intended thoughts and feelings onto him. Non-organic beings also intervene in the mind's body and cell management unit tasks, causing illness and disorder. Therefore, these beings can also be called "non-organic viruses."

1. Disorders Caused by Non-organic Beings

We can categorize disorders caused by the possession of a person's mind by non-organic beings as follows.

Mental Disorders

Sensory Hallucinations (visual, auditory, olfactory, somatic sensations): the individual hears sounds, sees objects or people that others do not notice, or has false feelings of, for example, being rejected by others or being constantly followed.

Imposed Hallucinations: imposed thoughts or mentation from non-organic viruses that result in development of unreal beliefs and assumptions or commands for unusual behavior displayed in a conscious state with no logical or emotional justification by the individual.

Multiple Personality Disorder: the presence of two or more personalities in an individual.

Bipolar Disorder: a condition in which a person rapidly goes back and forth between very good mood and depression.

Obsessive Compulsive Behavior: a condition in which an individual has unwanted and repeated thoughts, ideas, feelings or behaviors that drive him to do something.

Irrational Fears or Phobia: a persistent fear of an object or a situation. The individual suffering from phobia goes to great lengths to avoid the subject of this fear.

Hyper Activity Disorder (ADHD): a condition with over-activity, impulsiveness, inattentiveness or a combination.

Unusual Inclinations: unusual emotions, the urge to commit suicide, and causing harm to the self or others

Unusual Behaviors: sleep walking

Psychological Disorders

depression, anxiety, agitation, sense of guilt, and the like.

Physical Disorders

incurable diseases, genetic disorders, and the like.

Physical Mental Psychological Disorders

sleep quality disorders and the like.

Disorders with Unknown Causes

unexplained random bruises, swelling, wounds, scratches on the body, sleep walking (where the individual is guided around barriers or objects with closed eyes), sleep talking and screaming, bruxism, movement of pain over the body, sleep paralysis, and the like.

Non-organic beings in the first instance have their most destructive effects on the mind, and subsequently on the psyche, and finally on the physical body. Currently, neither modern medicine nor complementary medicine have any fundamental and definite treatments for the disorders and discomforts caused by these viruses. The common methods of treatment for these disorders are mainly to relieve the symptoms, thus masking but not resolving the problem, because we lack knowledge about the key factors causing the symptoms and the means of removing them.

2. Signs of Infection by Non-organic Beings

The aforementioned mental, psychological, and physical disorders describe only a fraction of various signs and symptoms of infection by non-organic beings. Other signs that indicate such infection include:

-Unusual inclinations and behavior

-Telepathy

-Reports of experiences in the state of hypnosis (that are often used in support of the theory of reincarnation)

-Abuse and taking advantage of non-organic beings

Unusual Inclinations and Behavior

Type B non-organic beings have strong effects on a person's life that include causing unusual inclinations and behavior. Although Type A can motivate these inclinations and behavior, Type B can more effectively cause people to manifest them.

Generally, an individual's sudden and non-discretionary change of inclinations and behavior to inclinations and manners of a recently deceased relative (usually nearly immediately after the relative's death) indicates the deceased relative's intervention in the individual's management system (mind).

For instance, after a father's death, the son noticeably exhibits one of the father's characteristics or habits. This behavior occurs because the deceased parent's mind body, due to his attachments and need for mental satisfaction, possesses the mind of his son, and thus, willingly or unwillingly, transfers his characteristics, inclinations, and illnesses to the host body.

Type B's reasons for choosing an individual vary. Being a family member, a friend, or a loved one is not required for this selection. In addition to the deceased person's feelings of love or hatred as a motive for possessing an individual, other factors can motivate this selection. Type B may choose a host with a specific similarity, such as a common interest or trait. Their choice might be based on their needs and what they lacked in life before death. They may target individuals capable of achieving their unfulfilled goals and dreams. To find someone with these qualities, they look beyond their friends and relatives. Some Type B viruses, without no consideration or hesitation, simply take their first opportunity of possession, with no preference for a specific person or characteristic.

In most such scenarios, the new inclination, characteristic, or trait that the possessed individual displays appears unusual to him and those around him.

Telepathy

A strong emotional bond between individuals results in connections between their mind bodies that open the door for transfer of non-organic beings from one person to another. This allows movement of the viruses from one person to the next. Thus, the virus is active between two or more individuals and is called a "Shared Virus". Generally, individuals with shared viruses sense each other's feelings and thoughts with no external or physical interactions. This state is commonly called "telepathy."

Telepathy often occurs between identical twins because they share a strong emotional bond. Further, because transfer of non-organic beings is equal during their mothers' pregnancy, they are infected by shared viruses that persist after birth.

Two individuals sharing love provides an opportunity for development of shared viruses. In the path of love, the lover and the beloved, attain unity to develop true empathy. For humankind to develop awareness about the existence of an intelligent bond between people and an intelligent bond among all elements of the universe, the experience of love is very valuable. Although this experience is undeniably essential on our path to *Kamal,* it can provide a means for viruses to transfer from one or both parties to the other and cause telepathic abilities.

Note that strong mental and emotional attention only creates an opportunity for the transfer of viruses. When neither party feels an urge to gain information about the other party's mental state, emotional state, or incidents surrounding him, non-organic viral transfer does not occur. However, other means of transmitting shared non-organic viruses include genetic transfer and non-organic beings casting spells that involve two or more individuals.

When a non-organic virus is shared between atleast two individuals, one party's attempt to evict the virus can, given distance and unawareness of such act, provoke the virus's reaction against eviction in the second person. In some experiences, successful elimination in one individual terminated all telepathic abilities.

In sum, telepathy can result when non-organic viruses exploit special mental or emotional attention between people, and so it reveals infection by these viruses.

Reports Given in the State of Hypnosis

The theory of reincarnation is thousands of years old, and billions of people believe in it. According to this belief, humankind is reborn into this world in a new body after our biological death. Different schools of thought have diverse ideas about the process of reincarnation. This rebirth can be in human, animal, plant, or solid form. Based on this belief some of those who die, instead of repeated return to this world, find eternal peace and are free from the reincarnation cycle.

The principle of karma underpins reincarnation. This principle holds that the consequences of people's actions are not lost and we experience the karma of our actions in two stages: first in this lifetime and second in our next life in this world. Thus, followers of reincarnation believe that each individual faces the result of his actions in his return to this world and burns off negative karma. People believe that this process occurs through a good person's rebirth into better life conditions such as a wealthy family and the rebirth of someone with negative karma into a lower life form (an animal, plant or an object) or a more difficult and challenging human life such as a very poor family so that the pain and suffering will facilitate karma burn-off.

For this reason, believing in reincarnation on one hand causes false judgment about poor and less fortunate people, taking them as sinners in past lives and deserving hardship and misery, and on the other hand favors the class system by accepting poverty and the superiority of wealthy and fortunate people in society.

With humankind's constant rebirth and continuous resulting karma burn-off, one would expect evolution in the quality of human nature. Although to date human intelligence has increased and our technological advancement is unprecedented, negative consequences of such developments are also growing. For instance, people of the current era can damage the environment as much as all earlier people combined. Therefore, not only do we not witness a reduction of the negative inheritance of one generation from the previous generation, but human life has also become more challenging and problematic than before. Therefore, it is difficult to accept that reincarnation has or ever will reduce negative karma.

Furthermore, it is incorrect to think that the plan of creation considers humankind as an eternal convict condemned to a repeating cycle of life in this world to burn off the negative karma of our mistakes and wrong-doings. Each individual can experience transformation in this lifetime to achieve *Kamal,* and God is gracious and would not refuse us the opportunity for such transformation. If the method of making amends for mistakes is another life in this world, and humankind's life is thus spent without a higher purpose, the plan of creation would seem pointless.

In addition, if we accept that humankind enters this world at birth, and after death a number of them are transformed into animals, plants, or objects and a small number of them achieve eternal peace and freedom from the reincarnation cycle, the world's human population would decrease. Further, if we accept that humankind enters this world from a different place, we should also easily accept that a different place exists after death. It would be easy to then believe that we leave this world forever for another realm where life is also possible.

With regard to the idea of humankind's rebirth in solid or object form, we must raise the question as to the proportional unit of solid form to which each human being returns. For instance, how much stone does the death of an individual who is to be reborn as stone create? Does he return as a rock or a mountain? Can we even consider a unit of measurement for stone? The theory of human rebirth in solid form fails to answer these questions, and so we cannot prove or accept this theory.

A significant point to note here is that the distinctive factor between humankind and other beings in this world is Humankind's "self[1]"

1- An equivalent to the Arabic word Nafs (نفس)

which in essence is different from all else that exists in this world. The origin of all beings including their software components is logic and only humankind's self is a result of love and is of such essence. In this world, no vessel other than the human body can develop the capacities of self and prepare the ground for manifestation of our free will.

The idea of reincarnation portrays for humankind a destiny of eternal pain–a suffering that, even if one becomes free of it, proves a pointless and purposeless plan of creation and demonstrates that the designer has created the material world in vain with no objectives nor direction.

However, one of the references often used to prove the idea of rein-carnation is the reports of a different life by subjects in the state of hypnosis. These reports seem to describe clear memories of events and incidents of a life with different geographical location, date, race, lan-guage, education, job, and gender. It is important that post-experiment investigations for certain cases have validated the identity of the indi-vidual reported. Sometimes, the hypnotized person even speaks the language of the person while telling his life story.

We argue, however, that these statements fact come from Type B viruses who have possessed the mind of the hypnotized individual. They have li-ved the lives they describe and are not telling stories of the host's past lives. Through hypnosis they communicate and reveal their existence. One sign of infection by non-organic viruses is the presence of such reports which end with eviction of the viruses, thus demonstrating that the statements do not represent the individual's past life memories.

Exploiting Non-organic Beings

Although people can obtain abilities such as seeing the future, reading one's thoughts and personality, imposing one's will on others, and prying into these areas by connecting to the negative network, it is also possible to gain such powers by associating with and taking advantage of non-organic beings.

Type A non-organic beings that participate in such acts are often Captivation Keepers. These beings make themselves available to those who wish to acquire the aforementioned powers to obtain what seems to be beneficial information for helping, sabotaging, or otherwise subliminally manipulating the lives of others.

We can divide information received from these beings into the following categories:

1. Seeing the future

2. Reading thoughts

3. Reading personalities

4. Knowing the hidden (details of private life, inner feelings and confidential affairs of others)

5. Cosmic awareness and *Kamal* awareness

Not only is gaining insight in the first four categories (direct from the negative network or with the help of non-organic beings) not *Kamal* oriented, but also insight into cosmic awareness and *Kamal* awareness, that in their essence are vital for humankind's journey, gained from these beings is not in the direction of *Kamal* because the consequences of any interactions with these non-organic beings are very severe for human beings.

Awareness that is useful for attaining *Kamal* is insight about God, self, and the material world. Only if attained on the step of love, this type of awareness has lasting effects that persist even after death and is valuable as *Kamal* awareness that becomes embedded in humankind's being. If attained through these beings, it is mere information. Further, attaining true insight about the material world (revealing secrets of what is also called the seven layers of the universe) is impossible for non-organic beings, so any insight they provide into theism, self-realization, and cosmology cannot exceed what humankind already knows.

Individuals may appoint one or more Type A non-organic beings as their agents to use their knowledge and receive answers to their questions, but they are unaware that these beings' answers and knowledge has been acquired from other people. More importantly, they are unaware that the non-organic beings are slowly imposing their own will and influence upon them.

Any decisions that people make on the basis of information from these beings may have serious and irreparable consequences on their lives. Not only because seeing the future, thoughts, and private information of others is not in the direction of *Kamal*, but also because such insights are not always based on truth or reality, and could be false information.

Humankind is generally exposed to two types of awareness:

Awareness in the Positive Direction (Kamal Oriented)	Awareness in the Negative Direction (Anti-Kamal Oriented)
Awareness in the direction of:	Awareness in the direction of:
- Realization and understanding of *Kamal*	- Gaining power and superiority over others
- Whyness of the creation and the purpose of being	-Reading personalities
- Ways to resolve conflicts and reaching unity	- Encouragement for judgment of others and pushing them towards multiplicity
- Insight about the unity of the universe	- Gaining powers such as mind reading, telling the future and exerting influence on others (imposing thoughts onto others)
- Sense of presence	
- Purpose for creation of humankind	- Encouraging selfishness and self-centeredness
- Creating feelings of hope, peace, serenity and joy	- Arousing feelings of disappointment, fear, anxiety, loneliness and sadness
- Magnificence of the Beloved	

One of the ways by which Type A non-organic beings engage in fortune-telling and divination is scrying. Humankind's interest in reflective surfaces like mirrors results from our interest to controlling a virtual reality. This interest can lead to opening a channel into the negative or positive networks, and essentially the mirror can reflect a manifestation of God or Satan.

A person considers virtual reality that which he can control. If he stares into the mirror, it reflects his virtual reality for the purpose of seeing the future or events in the past, non-organic beings engage in the individual's ultra-mind system and cause the desired images to appear before him.

In some cases, the mirror captures Captivation Keepers to reveal the desired information. Throughout history, kings and high-powered people in society held seers and fortune tellers in high esteem. Certain seers held their non-organic agents and mirror together, controlling the mirror and thus gaining insight into the future and the past.

However, in some instances, through the interference of the positive network or the radiational intrusion of their enemies (via witchcraft), they obtained false information upon which powerful people made important decisions that caused their collapse. Thereby, they entered a radiational war that usually turned out badly for them.

Non-organic beings can increase creativity. Type B viruses increase the possessed individual's enthusiasm and drive and thus increase negative or positive creativity. For instance, when a thief's mind body captures another thief's mind, the host becomes more skillful in robbery, which in turn is encouraged to find new ways to commit this crime.

Type A viruses however, do not stimulate creativity, and playing their role through intelligent methods does not result from their creativity because they cannot become inspired. They have only limited abilities within the boundaries of their role in the material world, and can choose to apply methods only within these boundaries.

Chapter 3

CAUSES OF INFECTION
BY NON-ORGANIC BEINGS

1- Common Causes

Various factors contribute to and cause humankind's infection by non-organic beings, including common factors that cause infection by both Type A and B viruses. Other causes of only Type A infections will be discussed in the Specific Causes section. The common factors include:

- Being in a negative state
- Addiction
- Taking advantage of non-organic beings
- Being under the influence of spell or magic
- Incoherency of human bodies
- Transmission from parents

Being in a Negative State

The most crucial condition that makes humankind susceptible to possession by non-organic viruses is being in a negative state such as fear, panic, anger, sadness, grief, anxiety, and despair. When one is in negative state, the negative radiation absorption and emission section of our psyche (psychological body) is open, making us vulnerable to possession by both Type A and B non-organic viruses.

This condition is so fundamental that even for a spell or magic to be activated, the individual must first be in a negative state. Therefore, one cannot argue that humankind is condemned to be captured by these viruses and has no role in our possession by these beings. Unless we are in a negative state, no spell or magic can affect us. The non-organic agents that activate spells have no means of possessing the individual's mind in a positive state. So each person is responsible for keeping his entire being safe in a positive state, lest he become vulnerable in negative state.

Falling into a negative state can happen in many ways. For instance, watching a horror movie can cause fear. Fear opens the metaphorical lid over the negative radiation absorption and emission section of psyche. As a result, not only can the individual be possessed by Spell Keepers and Captivation Keepers but also by Type B non-organic beings eager to possess the individual's mind. Consequently, the mind's commanding unit suffers from disorders and transmits various obvious and subliminal commands that affect the individual's health, thoughts, behavior, and speech.

Grief over a deceased loved one or a family member can also cause a negative state. This grief often reaches its peak during the funeral and burial in the cemetery, where many Type B viruses are present, increasing the chances of infection. In general, being in a cemetery while in a negative state increases our vulnerability to infection by Type B non-organic viruses.

Addiction

Addiction is a physical or mental dependency on a habitual action that causes symptoms beyond tolerance when suddenly stopped. Such symptoms make the addict feel helpless to stop, and so he continues the habit.

Addiction creates a kind of faulty information loop in the mind. As a result, the individual's various bodies crumble and fall into disarray, causing gaps through which non-organic beings can breach his mind. Most such beings belong to Type B non-organic beings wishing to participate in the person's experience (such as using an addictive substance).

Addiction to some drugs causes disorder in the reality assessment sensors of the brain, and the data transmitted to the brain through the five senses are assessed incorrectly to the extent that a drug addicted individual may develop distorted perception of size, volume, and distance. This misperception may not only lead the addict to misinterpret people or objects observed, but may even persuade the individual to jump from a height of, for example,100 m, thinking it is only 1 m. Impaired reality assessment sensors activate other sensors that increase the chances of seeing the non-organic beings.

Addiction can be developed through conscious and unconscious processes. In a conscious process, the tendency for addiction develops and increases gradually. For instance, a person who initially starts smoking occasionally becomes addicted gradually and cannot easily stop the habit.

In an unconscious process, subliminal factors contribute to addiction development. One such factor is the mind bodies of deceased people who had a form of addiction before their death. These Type B beings can possess a susceptible individual's mind and lead him toward addiction. In this case, the affected individual follows an inclination towards addiction with no conscious decisions or clear explanations.

Furthermore, unconscious inclination toward addiction can occur under the influence of subliminal persuasive messages transmitted to the unconscious part of the mind from, for example, music. In other words, as there exists matter and anti-matter, energy and anti-energy, so also consciousness and anti-consciousness exist in the material world, and we are constantly exposed to them.

The human mind is very intricate and contains many strong protective filters. One such filters is the logic filter, which blocks any data it defines as illogical and contrary to one's beliefs. Yet another part of the mind can process any subliminal data it encounters. Therefore, the central unit of the mind has no limitations for comprehension of different languages, even subliminal messages behind words and texts (their anti-consciousness). Hence any input can affect the mind, and such influence becomes apparent in the individual's behavior.

Based on this principle, the entire data input received by the central unit of the mind, influences human behavior and inclinations toward the intended direction. Tendency toward addiction is an example of such change in behavior and interests.

Use and Exploitation of Non-organic Beings

Intentional or unintentional use of non-organic beings for the purposes of predicting the future, fortune telling, casting spells, or performing magic and similar matters also make one vulnerable to infection by non-organic beings. For instance, in the process of tea leaf, palm, or Tarot card reading, the reader establishes a connection with non-organic beings that can strongly affect the reader's life regardless of his intentions. In fact, it is not the forms that take shape in the cup, the images on the cards, or other reading accessories that provide the information for the reader. Instead, through the readers' will and enthusiasm, non-organic beings impart insight into the desired matters, and thereafter signs and symptoms appear indicating infection by these viruses.

Thus, many readers and fortune tellers have chaotic lives as non-organic beings control their affairs. Such viruses also affect customers who visit them for readings.

Spells and Magic

Direct exposure to a certain category of spell-casting materials and tools infused with non-organic viruses also cause certain viral infections. To cast these spells, codes consisting of characters, numbers, texts, or special writings (often meaningless) activate an associated non-organic virus to start its defined task.

People who are unaware of the infection risks of these practices approach practitioners of these fields, seeking help to achieve goals such as having their issues resolved or making others think kindly of them. They seek assistance, unaware that non-organic viruses will then gradually control their lives, and even though one of their problems might appear to be resolved, hundreds of other issues will follow.

Additionally, the very act of casting a spell or requesting one will ultimately enslave you to evil forces. Black magic is even worse as the practitioners are intentionally trying to hurt someone (for example, jeopardizing family life, work, or educational conditions, silencing enemies, or forcing or restraining another's behavior). Through such actions they become infected with not only Spell Keepers viruses but also Universe Keepers and Retribution Keepers attracted by the negative radiation that the practitioner's evil intentions generate.

Incoherency of Human Bodies

Humankind has various bodies such as the physical, mind, psychological and astral Bodies. When these bodies fail to function synchronously, a range of issues from minor disorders to impulsive insanity might occur. In this case, bodies begin functioning independently so that one might not remember ordinary routines or might easily lose one's temper or self-control over trivial matters. Alcohol consumption and drug use can also cause bodies to go out of sync, substantially increasing people's vulnerability to infection by non-organic viruses.

Transmission from Parents

People can become infected with non-organic viruses at conception, at birth, and at any time throughout their life. The father's non-organic viral infections transmission happens at conception and the mother's at birth, once the umbilical cord is clamped. Therefore, everybody is born with a degree of infection naturally inherited from parents. Sometimes these viruses exist concurrently in both child and parents. Such infection affects the "programmed self"[1] section of the baby's mind. In other words, we play no role in incurring viral infections of this type, as the transmission occurs automatically through parents who similarly inherited them from their ancestors.

This mode of transmission transfers various types of non-organic viruses, including Spell Keepers, from generation to generation. However, people obtain a great proportion of their viral infection throughout life via the "programmable self"[2] section of the mind.

2- Specific Causes

Certain factors of humankind's non-organic virus infection are specific to Type A non-organic beings. These factors enable Type A viruses to play their role in causing human infection. Chapter One introduced many of these factors, primarily:

- Ignorance of the unity and consistency of the material world

- Desecration of any part of the material world

1- Once a human being is born into this world, he has a collection of programmed parts that distinguish him from others. These programmed parts, unique in each individual, are called "Programmed self." Programmed self includes instinct, entity, foundation, guiding soul, gene, and the like.

2- Alongside the programmed self, there are collections of parts that are programmed throughout life called "Programmable Self". Programmable self is open to learning and based on the information obtained throughout one's life determines the way the programs of instinct, entity, foundation, genes and so on should be accessed.

- Emission of any negative radiation in the material world
- Causing corruption and destruction of any kind and preventing any part of the material world from flourishing and prospering
- Intentional and deliberate confrontation with *Kamal* and the path to *Kamal*.

Ignorance of the Material World's Unity and Consistency

The material world is the manifestation of the one Creator, and all its parts in harmony, consistency, and unity are a single reflection of the Creator. Thus, being a monotheist means seeing the unity of the material world, and considering any part of this world separated, detached, or independent results from unawareness of this unity and puts one in the realm of *shirk*.

From a different outlook, one who breaks the vow of "You alone we ask for help (for each and everything)" and takes refuge in someone or something other than the one Creator, is unaware of the unity of the material world and commits *shirk*.

To acknowledge any source or power other than the Creator, associating anything as equal to and giving His attributes to others besides Him opens humankind to infection by Type A non-organic beings. In most cases, depression indicates this infection in the individual.

Desecration of Any Part of the Material World

Considering that the material world is the manifestation of its Creator, each of its elements has a guardian of Type A non-organic beings. In the event that a person harms or desecrates any part of this totality, Universe Keepers will oppose him.

Consequently, even unnecessarily breaking a tree branch or disparaging any other being for amusement causes infection by these viruses. Only when a living being (such as weed or insect) causes damage or illness, or in the natural food chain where people need to eat other living beings to survive, is it not considered desecration and will not result in encountering Type A non-organic beings.

All natural organisms and processes are significant and play a role in the ecosystem. Therefore, humankind, with our incomplete awareness, cannot consider any of them insignificant or less significant than ourselves. No person, based on his personal preferences, can overlook their importance and violate them. Any negation or refusal of their value and their sanctity is considered blasphemy. Humankind must recognize that any being in this material world is a face of its Creator and should walk on earth with respect and appreciation.

Emission of Negative Radiation

To disrespect a human being or to violate anyone's rights is a desecration of a part of the material world. Disrespect can appear as lie, by defaming someone, or by false accusation of another person. Committing these offenses emits a form of negative consciousness radiation that attracts Type A non-organic beings toward the offender.

For instance, although one might be feeling good and positive while speaking ill of someone in their absence, one's emission of negative radiation attract these viruses toward the individual and present an opportunity for them to possess the individual's mind.

Consciousness radiation consists of neither matter nor energy. It is not quantitative but is beyond time and space. Therefore, any offense creates negative consciousness radiation that affects the entire universe. In other words, every human offense and wrongdoing causes consciousness pollution, incurring invasion by non-organic beings.

Causing Corruption and Destruction

Preventing the flourishing and prospering, or causing corruption and destruction, of any part of the universe desecrates creation and releases negative radiation.

Any wastage or inappropriate usage of any element of existence or any actions against any being's development or growth can be considered as corruption. For instance, if a piece of meat is left to rot, it is wasted, and when someone's enthusiasm for something is crushed, that person is prevented from flourishing; thus, both behaviors cause corruption and destruction. Even by complaining about the weather we cause corruption. We certainly cause corruption by denying the intelligence of the universe and the role of interuniversal consciousness and its applications. The concepts of blasphemy, *shirk,* and corruption are far more significant than we have yet realized.

www.ingramcontent.com/pod-product-compliance
Lightning Source LLC
Chambersburg PA
CBHW060054050426
42448CB00011B/2461